E-BOOK BY RICHINVESTMENTS HOLDINGS LLC

I0422907

REALITY

PREMIUM SPRING WATER

HOW TO START YOUR OWN BEVERAGE BRAND

DETAILED GUIDE TO BUILDING YOUR BRAND

CONTENTS

INTRODUCTION

WELCOME TO "HOW TO START YOUR OWN BEVERAGE BRAND" A COMPREHENSIVE GUIDE TO STARTING YOUR BEVERAGE BRAND.

In this ebook, we'll take you on a journey to discover the key steps and essentials to build a successful beverage brand. From defining distribution to your brand identity, marketing, and beyond, this guide aims to equip you with the knowledge and inspiration you need to embark on your entrepreneurial beverage venture. Let's Go!!!!!

CHAPTER I: UNDERSTANDING THE BEVERAGE INDUSTRY

IN THIS CHAPTER, WE'LL DELVE INTO UNDERSTANDING THE BEVERAGE INDUSTRY, IT'S CURRENT TRENDS, AND HOW YOU CAN POSITION YOUR BRAND FOR SUCCESS.

The Beverage Industry Landscape

Gain insights into the diverse beverage market, which includes alcoholic and non-alcoholic drinks. Learn about the subsectors such as soft drinks, energy drinks, juices, alcoholic beverages and more. Understand the global and regional trends, market size, and projected growth to identify potential opportunities.

Consumer Preferences & Market Trends

Stay updated on the latest market trends, changing tastes, and consumer preference. Analyze factors that influence beverage choices, such as sustainability, health and wellness, convenience, and flavor innovations. Identifying emerging trends will help you create products that resonate with your target audience.

Identifying Your Niche

Discover the importance of finding a niche within the beverage industry. Assess the competition and identify gaps in the market that your brand can fill. Whether it's a unique flavor profile, functional beverage,or a new approach to packaging, carving out a distinct identity can set your brand apart.

Learning from Successful Beverage Brands

Examine case studies of successful beverage brands and their journeys to prominence. Understanding their marketing tactics, strategies, and key decisions that contributed to their success.Learn from their achievements to apply valuable insights to your own brands.

Beverage Industry Challenges

Acknowledge the challenges that aspiring beverage entrepreneurs might face. From supply chain issues to changing consumer preferences understanding these challenges will prepare you to navigate potential obstacles.

Adapting & Staying Innovative

Explore the significance of innovation in the beverage industry. Discover how staying adaptable and open to change can help your brand remain relevant in a dynamic market.

Forecasting Market Potential

Learn how to conduct market research and use data to forecast your beverage brand's potential succes. Identify your target matket and assess demand to ensure a sustainable business plan.

Understanding the beverage industry is the foundation of building a successful brand. By gaining insights into market trends, consumer preference, and your brand's unique position, you'll be better equipped to create a beverage brand that not only meets consumer needs but also thrives in a competitive marketplace. Let's move forward to Chapter 2 and begin defining your beverage brand!

CHAPTER II: DEFINING YOUR BEVERAGE BRAND

IN THIS CHAPTER, WE'LL EXPLORE THE CRUCIAL PROCESS OF DEF YOUR BEVERAGE BRAND IDENTITY, SETTING THE STAGE FOR YOUR BRAND'S UNIQUE POSTIONING IN THE MARKET

Core Values, Mission, and Vision

Craft a compelling vision that outlines the long-term aspirations of your beverage brand. Define a clear and concise mission statement that articulates the goals and purpose of your brand. Identify core values that will serve as the guiding principles behind your brand's actions and decisions.

Consumer Insights and Target Audience

Understand your target audience deeply by conducting thorough market research. Gather consumer insights to comprehend their pain points, purchasing behavior, preference. Tailor your brand's offering to cater specifically to the needs and desires of your target consumers.

Brand Voice and Personality

Humanize your by defining it's voice and personality.

Decide on the tone, language, and communication style

that aligns with your brand's values and resonates with your target audience. A consistent brand voice builds loyalty

and trust among consumers.

Unique Selling Proposition (USP) and Differentiation

Identify the factors that make your beverage brand unique in the market. Develop a compelling Unique Selling Proposition (USP) that sets your brand apart from competitors. Your USP should clearly communicate what makes your beverages special and why consumers should choose them over others.

Brand Storytelling

Craft a captivating brand story that connects with consumers on an emotional level.

Share the inspiration behind your brand, it's journey, and the experiences or people that influenced it's creation. A compelling brand narrative can foster a deeper connection with your audience.

Brand Visuals and Identity
Design a visually appealing brand identity, including logo, color scheme, and typography. Eye-catching and consistent visuals reinforce brand recognition and help consumers associate specific qualities with your products.

Embracing Authenticity
Stay true to your brand's values and promises . Consumers appreciate authenticity and transparency, so ensure that your brand's actions align with the image you portray.

Evolution and Adaptability
Recognize that brand identity may evolve over time, and be open to adjustments that align with changing consumer preferences or market trends. Strive to maintain the essence of your brand while remaining adaptable to stay relevant.

Brand Guidelines
Establish clear brand guidelines that define how your brand should be represented across various touchpoints and platforms.Consistency in messaging and visuals builds brand recognition and trust.

Defining your beverage brand is a critical step in creating a strong foundation for your business. By understanding your target audience, unique value proposition, and
vision, you can build a brand that stands out in the market and resonates with consumers. In Chapter 3, we'll explore the exciting process of research and product development. Let's continue crafting your success in the beverage industry!

CHAPTER III:
RESEARCH AND
PRODUCT
DEVELOPMENT

IN THIS CHAPTER WE'LL DIVE INTO THE EXCITING WORLD OF RESEARCH AND PRODUCT DEVELOPMENT, WHERE YOU'LL LEARN HOW TO TURN YOUR BEVERAGE IDEA INTO A REALITY.

Conceptualization and Ideation

Kickstart the product development process by brainstorming and ideating different beverage concepts. Consider your unique selling proposition (USP), target audience, and market trends to develop innovation and appealing ideas.

Market Validation and Research

Conduct thorough market research to assess the demand for your beverage product. Analyze pricing, competitor products,and positioning. Validate your ideas through surveys, focus groups, and consumer feedback to ensure your product meets consumer needs.

Beverage Formulation and Taste Testing

Collaborate with beverage experts, nutritionists, and flavor scientists to create the perfect formulation for your beverage. Conduct taste tests with potential consumers to refine your flavor profile and ensure it aligns with your brand's identity.

Branding Integration and Packaging

Integrate packaging considerations into the product development process. Work closely with designers to create packaging that complements your brand identity and enhances the product's appeal on the shelf.

Testing and Prototyping

Develop prototypes of your beverage product for further refinement and testing. Assess factors like shelf stabilit, packaging durability, and consumer acceptance through feedback and sampling.

Safety Compliance and Health

Ensure that your beverage product complies with health and safety regulations. Work with experts to meet all the necessary requirements and conduct any lab tests.

Scaling Up Production

As you finalize your beverage product, plan for scaling up production. Consider the volume of production required to meet demand while maintaining product qualit.

Pricing and Cost Analysis

Conduct a comprehensive cost analysis to determine the pricing of your beverage product. Factor in prodution, ingredients, packaging , and distribution costs while setting a competitive yet profitable price.

Packaging Sustainability

Explore sustainable packaging options to align with environmentally conscious consumer preferences. Choose eco-friendly materials that reflect your brand's commitment to sustainability.

Continuous Improvement and Product Iteration

Embrace a culture of continuous improvement by seeking feedback and iterating on your beverage product. Stay open to making necessary adjustments based on consumer insights and market trends.

Research and Product Development lay the groundwork for the success of your beverage brand. By carefully crafting a product that appeals to your target audience and aligns with your brand identit, you're one step closer to carving a niche in the competitive beverage industry. In Chapter 4, we'll delve into the vital aspects of labeling and packaging. Let's keep crafting your success in the beverage world!

CHAPTER IV: THE FIRST IMPRESSION OF YOUR BRAND; PACKAGING AND LABELING

IN THIS CHAPTER, WE'LL EXPLORE THE CRUCIAL ROLE OF LABELING AND PACKAGING IN CREATING A STRONG FIRST IMPRESSION FOR YOUR BEVERAGE BRAND.

The Power of Packaging

Understand the significance of packaging as a powerful marketing tool. Packaging serves as the first point of contact with consumers and can significantly impact their purchase decisions. Explore how attractive and functional packaging can make your brand stand out on the shelves.

Aligning Packaging with Brand Identity

Ensure that your packaging design aligns with your brand's vision, target audience, and values. Consistent branding across packaging builds brand recognition and fosters a sense of trust among consumers.

Eye-catching Design Elements

Work with skill designers to create eye-catching packaging that reflects the essence of your beverage product. Utilize colors, typography, and graphics that resonate with your target audience and differentiate your brand from competitors.

Sustainable and Functional Package

Consider the practical aspects of packaging such as reseal ability, portability, and ease of use. Embrace sustainable packaging options that align with your brand's commitment to environmental responsibility.

Compliance and Legal Requirements

Familiarize yourself with labeling regulations and compliance standards. Ensure that all mandatory information, such as allergen warnings, nutrition facts, and ingredient list, are accurately displayed on the label.

Label Information and Design

Create an informative and visually appealing label that communicates your brand story and product

attributes effectively. Use clear and concise language to convey essential details to consumers.

Health Claims and Labeling

Understand the regulations surrounding health claims and marketing statements on beverage labels. Comply with guidelines to avoid misleading consumers with false or unverified claims.

Packaging Durability and Testing

Conduct testing bro ensure the durability and functionality of your packaging during storage, handling, and transportation. Durable packaging protects the integrity of your beverage product and maintains it's quality.

Packaging Innovations

Stay updated on packaging trends and innovations in the beverage industry. Explore new materials, printing techniques, and packaging formats that can elevate your brand's packaging.

Packaging Unboxing and Experience

Consider the overall packaging experience for consumers, including unboxing and product presentation. A memorable unboxing experience can leave a positive impression on customers and encourage repeat purcbased.

Remember, your packaging and labeling are a direct reflection of your brand's values and identity. By creating functional, attractive, and compliant packaging, you can make a lasting impression on consumers and establish your brand as a trusted and recognizable player in the market.

In Chapter 5, we'll guide you through the essential legalities and compliance aspects of starting your beverage brand. Let's keep crafting success for your beverage brand journey!

CHAPTER V: NAVIGATING COMPLIANCE AND LEGALITIES

IN THIS CHAPTER, WE'LL DELVE INTO THE CRUCIAL LEGALITIES AND COMPLIANCE ASPECTS THAT YOU NEED TO CONSIDER WHEN LAUNCHING YOUR BEVERAGE BRAND.

Business Registration and Structure
Choose the appropriate legal structure for your beverage business, such as a sole proprietorship, LLC, partnership, or corporation. Register your business with the relevant government authorities and obtain the necessary permits and licenses to operate legally.

Safety and Health Regulations
Familiarize yourself with health and safety regulations applicable to the beverage industry. Ensure that your beverage production, storage, and handling processes meet the required standards to ensure consumer safety.

FDA and Regulatory Compliance (if applicable)
If your beverage falls under the jurisdiction of the Food and Drug Administration (FDA), comply with the relevant regulations and labeling requirements. This includes adhering to guidelines for nutritional information, health claims, and ingredient declarations.

Alcohol Beverage Licensing (for alcoholic beverages)
If you plan to produce and sell alcoholic beverage, navigate the complex regulations related to alcohol beverage licensing.

Obtain the necessary permits and adhere to state and federal laws governing the production and sale of alcoholic drinks.

Intellectual Property and Trademarks
Protect your brand identity by registering trademarks for your logo, brand name, and any unique product names. Safeguard your intellectual property to prevent infringement and maintain brand exclusivity.

Reporting and Taxation
Understand the tax implications for your beverage business, including sales tax, excise tax (for alcoholic beverages), and income tax. Keep accurate financial records and comply with reporting requirements to avoid legal issues.

Labeling Compliance
Ensure that your beverage labels comply with all relevant labeling laws and regulations. Include accurate and complete information, such as allergens, ingredients, nutritional facts, and any required warnings.

Environmental Regulations
Adhere to environmental regulations and sustainability standards when choosing packaging materials and managing waste. Embrace eco-friendly practices to demonstrate your commitment to environmental responsibility.

Product Liability and Insurance

Protect your business from potential product liability claims by obtaining adequate insurance coverage. Product liability insurance can safeguard your brand from financial losses resulting from product-related issues.

Employment Laws and Labor Practices

Understand labor laws and regulations related to hiring employees, wages, working conditions, and employee rights. Comply with employment laws to ensure fair and ethical labor practices within your beverage brand.

Navigating legalities and compliance is an essential aspect of building a successful and sustainable beverage brand. By adhering to laws, regulations, and best practices, you'll establish a strong foundation for your business and build trust with both consumers and authorities. In Chapter 6, we'll guide you through the exciting process of beverage production and manufacturing. Let's continue crafting success for your beverage brand journey!

CHAPTER VI: PRODUCTION AND MANUFACTURING

IN THIS CHAPTER, WE'LL EXPLORETHE CRITICAL STEPS INVOLVED IN BEVERAGE PRODUCTION AND MANUFACTURING TO BRING YOUR PRODUCT TO LIFE.

Choosing the Right Production Method

Evaluate various production methods available for your beverage, such as in-house production, contract manufacturing, or co-packing. Consider factors like production volume, equipment costs, and expertise required to make an informed decision.

Sourcing High -Quality Ingredients

Select the freshest and finest ingredients for your beverage formulation. Build relationships with reputable suppliers who can consistently provide the quality you desire.

Beverage Production Facilities

If you decide on in-house production, plan and set up a suitable production facility. Ensure it meets health and safety standards and has the necessary equipment for efficient production.

Quality Control and Testing

Implement stringent quality control measures to maintain product safety and consistency. Regularly conduct product testing to ensure your beverage meets your quality standards.

Production Capacity and Scalability

Anticipate the future demand for your beverage and plan for scalability.

Assess your production capacity and consider potential expansion opportunities.

Packaging Integration

Integrate packaging considerations into the production process. Work closely with packaging suppliers to ensure the packaging aligns with your beverage's production requirements.

Inventory Management

Establish effective inventory management practices to avoid stockouts and excess inventory. Monitor inventory levels and plan production accordingly.

Supplier Relationships

Cultivate strong relationships with ingredient suppliers, packaging vendors, and equipment providers. Reliable suppliers are crucial for a smooth and successful production process.

Efficient Production Processes

Optimize your production processes to maximize efficiency and minimize waste. Continuous improvement in production can lead to cost savings and improved product quality.

Food Safety and Compliance

Adhere to food safety regulations and compliance standards throughout the production process. Train staff on proper handling and sanitation practices.

Navigating the production and manufacturing stage requires careful planning and attention to detail. By choosing the right production method, sourcing high-quality ingredients, and maintaining rigorous quality control, you can ensure that your beverage product meets consumer expectations and regulatory requirements. In Chapter 7, we'll explore strategies for building a robust distribution network for your beverage brand. Let's comtinue crafting success for your journey in the beverage industry!

CHAPTER VII: BUILDING YOUR BEVERAGE BRAND'S DISTRIBUTION NETWORK

IN THIS CHAPTER, WE'LL DELVE INTO THE CRUCIAL PROCESS OF BUILDING A ROBUST DISTRIBUTION NETWORK TO REACH YOUR TARGET MARKET EFFECTIVELY.

Distribution Channel Analysis
Evaluate different distribution channels available for your beverage brand, such as retail stores, supermarkets, convenience stores, online platforms, and specialty stores. Identify the most suitable channels that align with your brand positioning and target audience.

Selecting Distribution Partners
Forge strategic partnerships with distributors, wholesalers, and retailers. Choose partners who share your brand's values and have a strong presence in your target markets.

Direct-to-Consumer (D2C) Strategies
Consider implementing direct-to-consumer (D2C) strategies to build a closer relationship with your customers. Create an online store and engage in personalized marketing to enhance the customer experience.

International and Regional Expansion
Plan for international and regional expansion if your distribution network. Conduct market research to identify potential growth opportunities in new markets.

Supply Chain Management
Streamline your supply chain management to ensure efficient product distribution. Optimize logistics, warehousing, and transportation to minimize lead times and costs.

Building Retailer Relationships
Nurture strong relationships with retailers to secure prime self space and gain visibility. Offer promotional support and incentives to encourage retailers to stock your beverage product.

E-Commerce and Online Sales
Leverage e-commerce platforms to expand your distribution reach. Develop a user-friendly website and utilize digital marketing to drive online sales.

Regional Sales Representatives
Consider employing regional sales representatives to promote your beverage brand in specific geographic areas. Sales representatives can build relationships with retailers and drive sales growth.

Sampling and Demo Programs
Implement demo and sampling programs to introduce your beverage product to potential customers. Allow consumers to taste your product firsthand, creating a memorable experience.

Analyzing Distribution Performance
Regularly assess the performance of your distribution network. Use data analytics to track sales, identify opportunities for improvement, and make data-driven decisions.

Building an effective and efficient distribution network is essential for the success of your beverage brand. By selecting the right distribution channels, forming strategic partnerships, and focusing on customer engagement, you can ensure that your products reach the hands of consumers and gain visibility in the market. In Chapter 8, we'll guide you through the exciting world of marketing and branding strategies to promote your beverage brand. Let's continue crafting success for your journey in the beverage industry!

CHAPTER VIII: EFFECTIVE BRANDING AND MARKETING STRATEGIES

IN THIS CHAPTER, WE'LL EXPLORE THE ESSENTIAL BRANDING AND MARKETING STRATEGIES TO CREATE A STRONG PRESENCE FOR YOUR BEVERAGE BRAND IN THE MARKET.

Creating a Comprehensive Marketing Plan
Develop a well-structured marketing plan that outlines your brand's goals, target audience, key messages, and marketing tactics. Your plan should encompass both traditional and digital marketing strategies.

Building a Strong Online Presence
Establish a captivating website and utilize social media platforms to connect with your audience. Engage in content marketing, including blog posts, videos, and infographic, to share valuable information and showcase your brand personality.

Social Media Marketing
Leverage the power of social media platforms to engage with your audience, build a community, and drive brand awarenes. Utilize platforms such as Instagram, Twitter, Facebook, and TikTok to share visually appealing content and interact with consumers.

Influencer Marketing
Collaborate with influencers and key opinion leaders who align with your brand's values and target audience. Influencer partnerships can amplify your brand's reach and credibility.

Content Marketing Strategies
Develop a content marketing strategy that entertains, educates, and adds value to your audience. Share engaging and shareable content that resonates with consumers.

Promotional Events and Sampling
Organize sampling events and promotional campaigns to give consumers a firsthand experience of uour beverage. Create memorable experiences that leave a positive impression on attendees.

Media Coverage and Public Relations
Engage with the media to secure press coverage and PR opportunities. Positive media exposure can boost your brand's reputation and visibility.

Loyalty Programs and Customer Engagement
Implement loyalty programs and customer engagement initiatives to foster repeat business. Reward loyal customers and encourage referrals to drive word-of-mouth marketing.

Co-Branding and Collaborations
Explore co-branding opportunities and collaborations with other brands to expand your reach to attract new customer segments.

Effective branding and marketing strategies play a pivotal role in the success of your beverage brand. By crafting a compelling brand story, engaging withyour audience through social media and content marketing, leveraging influencer partnerships, you can build brand awareness and loyalty. In Chapter 9, we'll delve into communifty building and customer retention strategies. Let's continue crafting success for your journey in the beverage industry!

Analytics and Monitoring
Monitor the performance of your marketing efforts using analytics and data tracking tools. Use insights to refine your strategies and focus on the most effective marketing channels.

CHAPTER IX:
ENGAGING YOUR COMMUNITY AND BUILDING LOYALTY

IN THIS CHAPTER, WE'LL EXPLORE THE VITAL ASPECTS OF ENGAGING WITH YOUR COMMUNITY AND BUILDING LONG-LASTING CUSTOMER LOYALTY FOR YOU BEVERAGE BRAND.

The Power of Community Building
Understanding the importance of community building in establishing a loyal customer base. Cultivate a sense of belonging and shared values among your customers.

Authentic Communication
Engage in authentic and transparent communication with your community. Respond to customer feedback, inquiries, and concerns promptly and sincerely.

Social Media Interaction
Actively participate in conversations on social media platforms. Acknowledge and appreciate your community's contributions and celebrate their engagement with your brand.

User-Generated Content (UGC)
Encourage and feature user-generated content from your community. Share photos, videos, and testimonials from satisfied customers to showcase the real-life experiences with your beverage.

Customer Surveys and Feedback
Regularly seek feedback from your community through surveys and polls. Use the insights gained to improvet your products and services based on their preferences.

Exclusivity and Personalization
Offer personalized experiences and exclusive perks to your loyal customers. Reward their loyalty with special promotion, early access to new products, or exclusive events.

Loyalty Programs and Rewards
Implement a loyalty program that incentivizes repeat purchases and referrals. Reward loyal customers with points, discounts, or exclusive gifts.

Customer Service Excellence
Prioritize exceptional customer service. Train your team to handle customer inquiries and resolve issues professionally and courteously.

Collaborative Initiatives
Involve your community in decision-making processes through focus groups and polls. Demonstrate that their opinions and preferences matter to your brand.

Environmental and Social Initiatives
Engage your community in social and environmental initiatives aligned with your brand's values. Communicate your brand's commitment to making a positive impact on society and the environment.

Building a loyal and engaged community is a continuous process that requires genuine care and dedication. By actively listening to your customers, valuing their contributions, and offering personalized experiences, you can foster a loyal customer base that advocates for your beverage brand.
In Chapter 10, we'll explore financial planning and funding options to support the growth of your beverage business. Let's continue crafting success for your journey in the beverage industry!

CHAPTER X: FINANCIAL PLANNING AND FUNDING OPTIONS

IN THIS CHAPTER, WE'LL EXPLORE THE ESSENTIAL ASPECTS OF FINANCIAL PLANNING AND FUNDING OPTIONS TO SUPPORT THE GROWTH AND SUSTAINABILITY OF YOUR BEVERAGE BUSINESS.

Creating a Detailed Budget
Develop a comprehensive budget that outlines all costs involved in starting and running your beverage brand. Consider expenses such as product development, packaging, production, marketing, distribution, and overhead costs.

Startup Costs and Initial Investment
Calculate the initial investment required to launch your beverage brand. Determine the source of funding for startup costs, whether it's from personal savings, loans or external investors.

Cash flow Management
Monitor and manage cash flow carefully to ensure that your business can meet it's financial obligations and maintain sufficient working capital.

Financial Projections and Forecasting
Create a realistic financial projections based on market research and sales estimates. Forecast revenue, expenses, and profits over the short-term and long-term.

Funding Options
Explore various funding options to support your beverage business, such as bank loans, lines of credit, angel investors, venture capital, or crowdfunding campaigns.

Self-Funding and Bootstrapping
Consider self-funding or bootstrapping as a means of financing your beverage brand. This involves using your personal savings or revenue generated by the business to cover expenses.

Angel Investors and Venture Capital

Seek funding from angel investors or venture capital firms that are interested in supporting innovative startups in the beverage industry.

Bank Loans and Lines of Credit

Approach banks or financial institutions to secure loans or lines of credit to fund your beverage business. Ensure that you have a solid business plan and financial projections to present to lenders.

Crowdfunding Campaigns

Consider launching a crowdfunding campaign on platforms like Kickstarter or Indiegogo to raise funds and build a community of early supporters.

Financial planning and securing adequate funding are crucial steps in ensuring the success of your beverage brand. By developing a solid financial plan and exploring various funding options, you can set your brand on a path of sustainable growth and profitability. In Chapter 11, we'll explore the significance of sustainability and ethical practices in the beverage industry. Let's continue crafting success for your journey in the beverage industry!

Grant Opportunities and Competitions

Look for grant opportunities or startup competitions that offer financial support to entrepreneurs in the food and beverage industry.

CHAPTER XI:SUSTAINABILITY AND ETHICS IN THE BEVERAGE INDUSTRY

IN THIS CHAPTER, WE'LL EXPLORE THE IMPORTANCE OF SUSTAINABILITY AND ETHICAL PRACTICES IN THE BEVERAGE INDUSTRY AND HOW THEY CONTRIBUTE TO THE SUCCESS OF YOUR BRAND.

Understanding Sustainability
Learn about the concept of sustainability in the beverage industry and it's impact on the environment, society, and economy. Understand the importance of reducing the carbon footprint and conserving natural resources.

Sustainable Sourcing of Ingredients
Emphasize the use of sustainably sourced ingredients for your beverage products. Consider working with suppliers who prioritize ethical and environmentally responsible practices.

Environmentally Friendly Packaging
Adopt eco-friendly packaging solutions to minimize waste and reduce the environmental impact on your brand. Explore biodegradable, compostable, or recyclable materials for your packaging.

Recycling Initiatives and Waste Reduction
Implement waste reduction and recycling programs within your beverage production and distribution processes. Aim to minimize waste and encourage recycling among your customers.

Water Conservation Practices
Conserve water resources in your production process and educate your consumers about the importance of water conservation.

Ethical Labor Practices
Ensure fair labor practices and uphold the rights and welfare of workers involved in the production and distribution of your beverage products.

Supporting Local Communities
Engage in initiatives that support and empower local communities where your brand operates. Partner with local organizations and suppliers to strengthen the local economy.

Social Responsibility Programs
Develop social responsibility programs that address important issues, such as pocerty, hunger, or access to clean water. Demonstrate your commitment to making a positive impact on society.

Communication and Transparency
Be transparent about your sustainability efforts and ethical practices. Communicate with your customers and stakeholders about your brand's initiatives and values.

Awards and Certifications
Consider obtaining certifications related to sustainability and ethical practices, such as Fair Trade or Organic certifications. Participate in awards and recognition programs that celebrate responsible brands.

By integrating sustainability and ethical practices into your beverage brand, you not only contribute to a better world but also gain a competitive edge in the market. Conscious consumers increasingly seek brands that align with their values, making sustainability a powerful differentiator. In Chapter 12, we'll explore common challenges faced by beverage entrepreneurs and strategies to overcome them. Let's continue crafting success for your journey in the beverage industry!

CHAPTER XII: OVERCOMING CHALLENGES AND STAY RESILIENT

IN THIS CHAPTER, WE'LL DISCUSS COMMON CHALLENGES FACED BY BEVERAGE ENTREPRENEURS AND STRATEGIES TO OVERCOME THEM, FOSTERING RESILIENCE ON YOUR JOURNEY TO SUCCESS.

Navigating Competitive Market Landscape
Understand that the beverage industry is highly competitive. Differentiate your brand through unique product offerings, exceptional branding, and excellent customer engagement.

Managing Cash Flow and Finances
Maintain a strong focus on financial planning and cash flow management. Build a contingency fund to handle unexpected challenges and maintain a healthy financial position.

Adapting to Change Consumer Preferences
Stay abreast of evolving consumer trends and adapt your products and marketing strategies accordingly. Be open to product innovation to meet changing demands.

Supply Chain Disruptions
Create a resilient supply chain and develop contingency plans to address potential disruptions in sourcing ingredients or packaging.

Brand Visibility and Marketing
Consistently invest in marketing efforts to build brand visibility and recognition. Embrace creative and cost-effective marketing strategies to reach your target audience.

Regulatory and Compliance Hurdles
Stay informed about the latest regulations and ensure full compliance to avoid legal issues. Seek professional advice when necessary.

Scaling Up Production

Plan for scalability as your brand grows. Monitor production processes and logistics to ensure smooth scaling without compromising quality.

Customer Loyalty and Retention

Focus on building strong customer relationships and providing exceptional customer service. Implement loyalty programs to retain existing customers and encourage repeat purchases.

Managing Brand Reputation

Monitor online reviews and feedback actively. Address customer concerns promptly and professionally to protect your brand's reputation.

Nurturing Resilience and Perseverance

Recognize that entrepreneurship is a journey with ups and downs. Stay resilient, remain adaptable, and learn from challenges as you progress. Embrace challenges as opportunities for growth and learning. Your beverage brand's success is a culminaction of determination, continuous improvement, and customer-centricity. By staying resilient and overcoming obstacles, you'll carve a path towards long-term success in the competitive beverage industry.

Congratulations on completing "How To Start Your Own Beverage Brand" Armed with the knowledge and strategies from this guide, you're ready to embark on an exciting and rewarding journey in the beverage industry. Remember, success is a result of passion, hard work, and a commitment to delivering value to your customers. Cheers to your future success!

CONCLUSION

THIS IS THE BEGINNING OF SOMETHING GOOD.

Congratulations! You've reached the end of "How To Start Your Own Beverage Brand". Throughout this guide, we've covered the essential strategies and steps to help you launch and grow a successful beverage brand. From understanding the beverage industry landscape to defining your brand identity, conducting product development and research, creating effective
marketing and branding strategies, and building a loyal community, you now have the tools and knowledge to craft your success in the competitive beverage market.
Remember, starting a beverage brand requires passion, dedication, and perserverance. Embrace challenges as opportunities to learn and grow,and always prioritize sustainability, ethical practices, and customer satisfaction.
As you embark on your entrepreneurial journey, stay focused on your vision, mission, and core values. Continuously innovate, adapt to changing trends, and listen to your customers' needs. Building a successful beverage brand is a
dynamic process that involves ongoing learning and improvement. The beverage industry offers countless possibilities for creativity and innovation. Whether you're creating refreshing beverages, functional drinks, or
artisanal concoctions, your commitment to quality and authenticity will set your brand apart.

Never forget that success comes from the love you put into your craft, the trust you build with your customers, and the positive impact you make on the world. Stay resilient, stay passionate, and remember that every challenge you overcome brings you closer to your goals. As you move forward, embrace the excitement of bringing your beverage brand to life. You have the power to quench thirsts, delight tastebuds, and leave a lasting mark in the hearts of your consumers.

So, raise your glass to a bright and prosperous future for your beverage brand. Cheers to your success, and may your brand continue to thrive, leaving a memorable impression in the world of beverages.
Best of luck on your journey, and may you craft a legacy of success in the beverage industry!

www.ingramcontent.com/pod-product-compliance
Lightning Source LLC
Chambersburg PA
CBHW020506290526
45786CB00005B/2009